Carolina Seashells
Nancy Rhyne

The East Woods Press

Library of Congress Cataloging in Publication Data

Rhyne, Nancy, 1926-
  Carolina seashells.

  Bibliography: p.
  Includes index.
  1. Shells—North Carolina. 2. Shells—South Carolina. I. Title.
QL415.N8R48   594'.0471'09756   81-17342
ISBN 0-914788-53-1   AACR2

Cover and illustrations by Steve Baldwin.
Typography by Raven Type.
Printed in the United States of America.

An East Woods Press Book
Fast & McMillan Publishers, Inc.
429 East Boulevard
Charlotte, NC 28203

About the Author

Nancy Rhyne has combed beaches from Portland, Maine to Acapulco, from Martinique to Curacao, and has found none more pleasing than the beaches of the Carolinas. She has done research and written articles for such national publications as *Town & Country* and *The New York Times*. Her first book, *The Grand Strand: An Uncommon Guide to Myrtle Beach and Its Surroundings* (East Woods Press, $4.95) is sold in bookstores.

About the Illustrator

Charlottean Stephen Baldwin is familiar in art circles in the Carolinas for his keen eye for detail and painstaking execution in water color and pen and ink. He is a naturalist at heart, and that, along with his love of the coast, gives his illustrations a special sensitivity.

I have seen
A curious child, who dwelt upon a tract
Of inland ground, applying to his ear
The convolutions of a smooth-lipped shell,
To which, in silence hushed, his very soul
Listened intensely; and his countenance soon
Brightened with joy, for from within were heard
Murmurings, whereby the monitor expressed
Mysterious union with its native sea.

Wordsworth

For Garry, who was that curious child

Acknowledgments

I wish to thank the following people for their invaluable help in this work:

Doris Ready of Paperback Booksmith at Myrtle Square Mall, Myrtle Beach, S.C., who said, "Nancy, write a book on Carolina seashells."

Sally Nunnally, Education Coordinator, Marine Resources Center, Fort Fisher.

Bruce Lampright of the Belle W. Baruch Institute for Marine Biology and Coastal Research, Georgetown, S.C.

And a very special thanks to the people at The East Woods Press, especially Sally Hill McMillan, Barbara Campbell and Linda Benefield, who helped me get the shells in this book in order. Now if she could only help me get my baskets, bowls, jars and boxes of shells in order.

Contents

Contents _____

Introduction

Seashells.

The very word starts with a smile and ignites the imagination.

Their colors and forms are myriad, and the price is right—free. Seashells have become popular objects of art for decorating. For example, graceful shells are the focal point of rooms in Nags Head and Hilton Head beach houses and in Myrtle Beach condominiums. Some of the country's top decorators found seashells just the right touch for apartments at the Olympic Tower on Fifth Avenue in New York. A seashell can be as lovely in living rooms, family rooms and recreation rooms as a Dali or Picasso. Shells magic what they touch, be it sand at the tideline or a mahogany table. The graceful curve of a seashell is the crown of nature's artistry.

Mother Nature creates, through the shells' evolution, for the world's great seas, timeless art treasures. No human craftsman, even if he labored hours and hours, could match the rich detail in the designs of seashells. Nature spawned the fantastic when she put shells to live on the floors of the seas.

Shell folklore

People have always been fascinated by seashells. They are found in ancient temples, graves and sacred statues. The remains of people who lived at the second town to be built at Jericho (between 6000 and 4500 BC) were found with eye sockets filled with seashells. Botticelli painted his famous picture of Venus, Goddess of Beauty, rising from the sea in a seashell. American Indians used scallop shells as dishes and made knives from the sharp lips of other shells. Shell cups and ornaments were used in their religious and war ceremonies. Some of these cups, made from the cores of certain shells, were buried with important people. Shells were sometimes placed on the top of Indian burial mounds.

The mollusks: bivalves and gastropods

Seashells are mollusks, which are defined as any invertebrate of the phylum *Molluska*, typically having a calcareous shell of one, two or more pieces that wholly or partly enclose a soft body. Mollusks are a major limb on the animal family tree. About 100,000 living forms have been found throughout the world. For the purposes of this book, mollusks are divided into two classes: bivalyia and gastropoda. Bivalves have a shell consisting of two pieces which are attached by muscles and teeth. (Bivalves are called "the clams.") Gastropoda have a single shell and are usually spiral. (Univalves are called "the snails.")

How shells grow

A shell is a structure made of lime taken from sea water by a mollusk as it fashions itself a splendid house. The development is started in the larval stage of the animal's life; some shells develop rapidly while others form more slowly. The rate of development depends on environmental factors. For instance, food influences a shell's structure. A food-rich environment helps some shells become thicker and more colorful.

A mollusk's internal organs are covered by a sac of skin called the mantle, and this is the organ that manufactures the shell. (The mantle is on the inside of a mature shell.) The mantle secretes a substance that mixes with carbonate of lime, which is obtained from the food supply. Bit by bit the shell is formed.

Color comes to the shell through rhythmic deposition of pigments in the mantle. Colors are spread over the shell in the form of lines, spots, stains, streaks, rays or stripes. A pigment fed to the shell at a certain time can produce a line of color spiralling around the shell. Sunlight and heat also influence color, and that is why some shells of the same species vary in color.

Fossil shells

Remains of ancient shells have been preserved in layers of rock forming the earth's crust, and these fossil shells give clues to the ages of the layers of earth. Good fossil-shell sites in the Carolinas are found where a cut has been made into rivers, streams or beaches. The banks of the Intracoastal Waterway, especially the Crescent Beach/Windy Hill-section near the North Myrtle Beach airport and the area near U.S. 317 opposite Grand Strand General Hospital, are excellent fossil hunting grounds in S.C. Specimens found in the banks of the Waterway in the Myrtle Beach area are estimated by marine scientists at the University of South Carolina to be about 2.5 million years old. All shells found there are fossils. Among species this writer has found in Waterway banks are quahog, cockle, ark, tulip, Scotch bonnet and murex. Fossil shells enhance any shell collection, and today many collectors restrict their collections to fossils only.

When you search for shells near the Waterway, try to time your search at a low tide. Waterway beaches are covered by water at high tide. Remember, there is a three-hour difference in Waterway and ocean tides.

The interiors of the shells encased in the banks of the Waterway are filled with hardened mud; however, the cementlike mud can be picked out, usually without harming the specimens. Many shells in private and public collections came from the banks of the Intracoastal Waterway. One such collection is on display at the Simeon B. Chapin Memorial Library at Myrtle Beach, S.C.

You can also look for fossil shells wherever the ground is being excavated in the coastal plain of South Carolina. Bulldozers often unearth fabulous specimens. One collector found 500 sharks teeth near Charleston where a power company was digging. Also near Charleston, the fossils of two whole whales were found in a ditch where a sewer line was being laid. It's a good policy to ask permission before going onto a site of commercial excavation to search for fossil shells.

Millions of years ago, the ocean covered the entire coastal plain of the Carolinas. There is a ridge of sand dunes at Shaw Air Force Base at Sumter, S.C. that is believed to have been the line of dunes that formed a ridge at the ocean's edge millions of years ago. Fossil shells are found in rivers, streams and at excavation sites as far inland as Sumter.

On the beaches: when and where to look

Although certain species are found only in special habitats, thousands of miles of sand beaches provide collecting grounds for many species. Malacologists (those who study mollusks) say the availability of shells has diminished in recent years. Hugh J. Porter, of the University of N.C. Institute of Marine Sciences at Morehead City and author of *Sea Shells Common to North Carolina*, points out that collectors have helped themselves to shells that washed ashore for more than a thousand years, and it will take a long time to restore the supply of shells. Arthur M.

LaBruce, of Pawleys Island, whose interest in shells went from hobby to business, said, "You don't find them as easily as in past years."

Just after a hurricane is a prime time to search for shells. Storms pull them from their ocean floor fossil beds and wash them to shore. Don't forget to examine wads of seaweed for shells that may be lodged within. It doesn't take a hurricane to wash seaweed up on the sand, and close examination is likely to produce some finds. You would need a magnifying glass to see some of the tiny shells bedded down in the seaweed, but if you shake the seaweed, many of the shells will fall onto the sand. You can watch them as they move about and, using their tiny feet, dig into the sand.

Some areas of the coast of the Carolinas have earned a reputation as the "best places" to find shells. In North Carolina, the best places include Cape Hatteras National Seashore, Ocracoke Island, Cape Lookout National Seashore and Shackleford Banks at the southern tip of Cape Lookout National Seashore. Hammocks Beach State Park near Bogue Sound and the swashes and inlets near Wrightsville Beach are good too.

When the tide flows out, people with picks and hammers crawl over a huge rock formation on the strand in Myrtle Beach, S.C. at 20th Avenue South and Ocean Boulevard. Wonderful shells and other creatures such as starfish are caught in the rocks when the tide recedes. Other "best places" in South Carolina include Huntington Beach State Park near Murrells Inlet, where the ocean throws excellent shells up on the sand, and the Kiawah Island beach, south of Charleston. Immediately after the onslaught of Hurricane David in 1979, near-perfect specimens were found scattered on this beach. Fine collections of sharks teeth have been found at the south end of Pawleys Island and at Litchfield Beach, just north of Pawleys.

If you look hard enough, you will find excellent specimens on all Carolina beaches, but LaBruce offered a word of advice: Don't go shelling when a south wind is blowing. There's something about a south wind. . . .

A crack time for collecting shells is the time of a new or full moon. Then, the sun and moon join forces, and the increased rise and fall of the tides result from the pull of the moon, and, to a lesser extent, the sun. Early spring and September are favorable times to gather shells in the Carolinas, but the tides bring shells all during the year.

Shell collections

Your collection of shells may not rival the 9 million specimens of the United States National Museum under the Smithsonian Institution in Washington, but once you have a collection, it is permanent. Shells retain their colors, and they do not decay. The beauty and value of a collection depends largely on the way the shells are cleaned and arranged for exhibit. Most shells can be cleaned of their animal parts by being boiled in fresh or salt water for about five minutes. The meat can then be extracted with a pin. (Delicate and fragile shells should be soaked until the animal parts float away.) After a shell has been cleaned, it is usually most attractive in its natural state, but for species that need brightening, a thin coating of mineral oil will restore subtle shades of color.

Most collectors put their shells in a case with a label near each specimen identifying it. The label states when and where the shell was collected and gives a brief description of the conditions under which it was taken. The value of a collection is proportional to the labeling of the shells. The precise locality and date are especially important. "Found on the Grand Strand" doesn't tell much. "Found on Jan. 2, 1983, at the low tide line, 1.5 miles south of the Pawleys Island pier, at 6:05 a.m." is an example of a good description. It also enhances a collection if the label shows the scientific name as well as the popular name of the specimen.

Since your collection may grow and become more valuable, you may choose not to glue your specimens permanently in the case. You never know when you will find a more perfect specimen to replace an existing one. Some collectors enjoy displaying driftwood, seaweed and other items from the sea within the case to create a natural setting, while others limit the exhibit to shells only.

Marine resource centers

The Office of Marine Affairs, North Carolina Department of Administration, provides three Marine Resource Centers on the coast of North Carolina at Roanoke Island, Bogue Banks and Fort Fisher. The centers serve as educational and research facilities, and courses offered to the public include "Fossils Along the Coast," "Shell Collection," "Shell Sketches" and "Shellfish Cookery." For more information on the centers and their programs, write to:

N.C. Sea Grant College Program
105 1911 Building
North Carolina State University
Raleigh, N.C. 27650

The Belle W. Baruch Institute for Marine Biology and Coastal Research offers courses at the Hobcaw Barony facility on U.S. 17, just north of Georgetown, S.C. "Shells and Fossils of the Lowcountry" is a course for "pack rat" beachcombers who want to identify their treasures and learn about the animals that once occupied the shells. For information, write the institute at P.O. Box 1630, Georgetown, S.C. 29440. A museum featuring shells and fossils will be open to the public in the spring of 1982.

700 species of shells in the Carolinas

More than 700 species of shells are found in or near Carolina estuarine and marine waters. This book describes those shells that are common enough to be found by the summer vacation collector. Some South Carolina species do not get as far north as Cape Hatteras, because South Carolina gets some Caribbean fauna that North Carolina doesn't receive. On the other hand, North Carolina receives some shells native to more northern regions that South Carolina does not get. But for the most part, the same shells that are indigenous to the North Carolina coast are found on the coast of South Carolina, though not every specimen can be found everywhere in this area. None of the shells in the pages that follow are indigenous only to the Carolina coast, and most of them are common to Atlantic beaches from Virginia southward or even from Massachusetts to Florida.

The most common classes of shells are Pelecypods, two shells that have a hinge-like closing, known as Bivalves (described in Part One), and Gastropods, one-shelled creatures known as univalves (described in Part Two). However, not all the shells commonly found on Carolina beaches are univalves or bivalves. The sand dollar, so common to Carolina beaches, is an echinoderm, closely related to the starfish. And rams horn shells are cephalopods. Part Three deals with other forms of sea life that are commonly collected on Carolina shores.

The size given for each species is usually the maximum size for specimens found on the coast of the Carolinas.

So many species were eligible for inclusion here that it is unlikely that all malacologists will be satisfied with the selection. My hope is that the reader will consider this book an introduction to the wide range of habitats in which mollusks can flourish and to the hundreds of species that have been found on the Carolina coast.

Part One
Bivalvia

Bivalves (Pelecpoda) have two shells (valves) that are attached by one or two strong muscles on the inside of the shells. Some of the shells have interlocking teeth at the hinge that work as a kind of spring, and the teeth resemble the teeth of a comb.

Bivalves have no mouth and no head. They feed by sucking into the inner chamber of the two shells decomposed animal, mineral and vegetable matter floating in sea water. They move along on a foot that protrudes from the shells.

Oysters, clams, cockles, mussels and scallops are some of the most common species of Carolina bivalves. Unless specimens are taken alive, the collector usually finds only one valve that washed to shore. These shells are usually bleached and have no outer layer. If a bivalve is taken fresh, the periostracum, a covering layer that is sometimes hairy, is often intact.

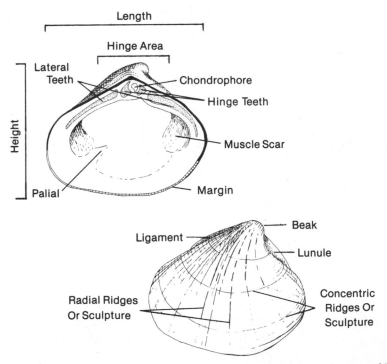

Coquinas

Coquina *(Donax variabilis)*

The tiny coquina (about ¾ inch) lives in shallow water. With the aid of a foot this wedge-shaped bivalve buries itself in loose sand near the mid-water line where sand fleas congregate. The sand fairly explodes with coquina as waves flow back into the sea after washing the sand from the animals buried there. Coquina can be scooped up by the handful just before they tunnel into the sand, and can be made into coquina chowder.

Coquina shells come in a bewildering variety of colors—rose, yellow, lavender, brown, red and lots of purple. Colorful bands spread out from the hinge muscle. When a coquina shell also has fine lines in a concentric pattern, and many do, the effect is a plaid design.

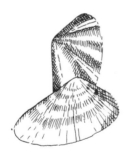

Coquina shells, opened like butterfly wings, naked and pure, decorate Carolina beaches. It is easy to find both valves intact, each with identical coloring. The inner portion of the shell is shiny and is often, though not always, deep purple. No polishing is needed to enhance these jewels of the sea.

Arks

On the most casual stroll along a Carolina beach, you are likely to find a passel of ark shells. The empty, bleached-white shells are scattered everywhere, but if you were to observe one alive in its native environment of ocean-bottom marine grass, it would be clothed in an outer layer of skin (periostracum) that is dark brown or black, often hairy and rather bristly.

There are plenty of arks on the beach for everyone, and the rippled shells are wonderful in a shell collection. Arks are somewhat squarish, unlike cockles which are similar but elongated or heart-shaped. A simple way to distinguish an ark from a cockle is to look for the ark's comblike teeth arranged in a line on both valves. (Cockles have a few widely-spaced cardinal teeth.) The arks you will reach for on Carolina beaches include:

Transverse Ark *(Anadara transversa)*

This little 1-inch shell, which is white inside and out, is oblong and has 12 strong ribs. If you were to find the two valves still attached, you would see that the two do not match perfectly; one laps a little over the other.

Blood Ark *(Anadara ovalis)*

This ark loves sandy bottoms and shallow water, and it gets its name because it has red blood. The blood ark, about 2 inches, is more oval in shape than some other arks. It is thick and solid, and about 35 ribs radiate from the beak area. This shell on northern shores is chalky white; its southern counterparts are somewhat shiny.

Mossy Ark *(Arca imbricata)*

Although the mossy ark looks much like the turkey wing, the sculpture on the surface of this brown shell is much finer grained. It also lacks the zebralike decoration of the turkey wing. A mossy ark grows to about 2½ inches, and if you saw one in the water alive, the mosslike outer layer would show you why its name is perfect. The margins, or edges, are smooth, which is not true of all ark shells.

Unlike most other shells, this one has red blood! Examine the numerous teeth at the hinge.

Bright Ark or White-Bearded Ark
(Barbatia candida)
This shell (up to 3 inches) is white. The thick places, where radiating ribs cross concentric lines, look like tiny beads. The anterior end is round, but the posterior is pointed. Hinge teeth are small.

Reticulate Ark
(Barbatia domingensis)
This ark lives happily in nooks and crannies of jetties and rocks in shallow water. It is 1 inch long, strong and rugged. Strong radiating ribs and concentric beads make a prominent crisscross pattern. It is yellowish white or off-white, and the edge is scalloped.

Adams' Ark (Arcopsis adamsi)
This tiny white or yellowish white clam, about ½ inch, is sometimes called Adams' miniature ark. It is adorned with thick beaded lines and is well inflated, almost rectangular in shape.

Turkey Wing (Arca zebra)
This bivalve with zebra stripes on its shell grows to 4 inches, but more often than not the ones you find will be about 2 inches. The beak at the hinge area curves inward, and the hinge line is straight with about 50 small teeth. This shell is white with a brown, zebralike pattern. The inside is lavender. Since this shell nips in a little at the center and flairs out at the sides in winglike fashion, it is easy to mistake it for a mossy ark, which has the same shape.

Incongruous Ark
(*Anadara brasiliana*)

The incongruous ark shell has about 25 well-defined ribs with grooves between them. The ribs are rigid and strong, and they are conspicuous on the inner shell. This ark grows to 2½ inches and lives in shallow water with gravel bottom. Its shell is white and considerably inflated—so full-blown, in fact, it seems short for its height.

Cut-ribbed Ark
(*Anadara lienosa floridana*)

For centuries Carolina tides have lapped over this shell, so abundant in ocean drift. Cut-ribbeds (3 to 5 inches) are white with a brown periostracum. About 35 radiating ribs widen as they approach the edge of this sturdy shell.

Ponderous Ark (*Noetia ponderosa*)

The ponderous ark loves sandy bottoms and shallow water. During its life it wears a layer of velvet black, but the shells you find on the beach are usually white. Its prominent beak turns inward, and the teeth are smaller at the beak area than at the ends of the dental ridge. This shell gets its name from its shape—massive, heavy and crammed with ribs. It grows to about 2½ inches.

Bittersweets

Bittersweets have a delicate decoration so nearly perfect it looks as if an artist drew it. Very uniform in size ribs go from hinge to margin of the almost round shell.

Lined Bittersweet
(Glycymeris undata)
This shell (about 1¾ inches) is of medium inflation. It is creamy white with irregular stains of brown. It is heavy, but smooth—almost silky. Radial ribs are separated by white lines. The inside is white with splotches of brown.

Combed Bittersweet
(Glycymeris pectinata)
About 20 or more substantial ribs spread out from the hinge on this bittersweet. This shell (1 inch) is gray white with splotches of yellow or brown.

American Bittersweet
(Glycymeris americana)
This shell (1½ to 5 inches) is not too common. It has five furrows and is circular and rather flat. The margin is somewhat scalloped, and the dorsal or hinge side is quite long. American bittersweet is tan with light yellow or brown stains.

Mussels

Mussel shells, bivalves whose two shells are the same size, are fan-shaped. The beak is at the narrower (anterior) end. The shells are thin and rather weak.

A mussel shell has a beard of threadlike filaments (byssus). With these strands the mussel anchors itself to rocks, piers or other hard surfaces. Although the mussel can release itself and move about, it would take a lot of force to pry it from its mooring.

Mussels are eaten in many countries (Europeans consider them a delicacy), but Carolina mussels generally are not eaten.

Common Blue Mussel
(Mytilus edulis)

This blue black shell (about 2 inches) is common north of Cape Hatteras but is rare south of the cape. It is long and slender (elongate), and the anterior edge is straight. The inside is white with lavender edges. Blue mussels can be seen attached to hard surfaces under the water or on pilings of wharves.

Paper Mussel *(Amygdalum papyria)*

As the name indicates, this 1-inch shell is fragile. Although the surface has fine growth lines, it is smooth. It is gray green or yellowish brown, and the inside is iridescent.

Tulip Mussel *(Modiolus americanus)*

This shell (2 to 4 inches) is thin and puffed up. The surface of the yellowish brown mussel is smooth, and the inside is purple.

Northern Horse Mussel
(Modiolus modiolus)

Here again is an oblong mussel that fastens itself to rocks offshore. This bivalve's shell (nearly 5 inches) is coarse and thick. It is pale lilac, but a brown leathery skin covers most of the shell. It is unfit for food.

Hooked Mussel
(Brachidontes recurvus)

The narrow side of this somewhat triangular shell (1¾ inches) is curved like a new moon. It is purplish gray, and the ribs radiate from the beak end.

Giant Date Mussel
(Lithophaga antillarum)

This shell can be more than 4 inches

long. It is thin and cylindrical, and the minuscule beak is low. The hinge line has no teeth. Numerous fine, concentric furrows decorate the surface. It is brown with a brown outer layer. For a secure home, this animal bores a hole in limestone and settles in.

Scissor Date Mussel
(Lithophaga aristata)

Believe it or not, this little shell has a calcareous increstation that extends beyond the posterior end, and this triangular shaped extension resembles the beak of a scissorbill bird. You can find this shell on Carolina shores, but it is more common south of the Carolinas. This rock borer grows to 1 inch. It is light brown.

Mahogany Date Mussel
(Lithophaga bisulcata)

A white calcareous deposit grows on this 1-inch shell. Cylindrical in shape, this mussel shell is brown. Two furrows spread from the beak to the posterior end of the shell.

Cinnamon Chestnut Mussel
(Botula fusca)

A tiny shell (½ inch) with strong, arched concentric growth lines, this gray brown mussel is a serious rock borer.

Ribbed Mussel (Geukensia demissa)

Radiating ribs decorate the ribbed mussel's yellow green or blue green shell. The inside is silvery. It is long and thin and grows to 4 inches.

Scorched Mussel
(Brachidontes exustus)

Resembling a little 1-inch fan, this shell

is ribbed on the surface and is blue gray. When alive, it sports a yellow brown outer covering.

Platform Mussel
(Congeria leucopheata)
This shell (about 1 inch) is classified a false mussel. In the beak cavity there is a little shelf where the muscle is attached. It is gray brown.

Pen Shells

The pen shell is unique, a work of art in its own right. Large and fragile, pen shells are fan-shaped. Byssal threads, which extend from the narrow end, help hold them in the sand, but the threads are not usually intact when a shell is found. According to legend in the Mediterranean countries, byssal threads from shells can be collected and woven into cloth. A gown fashioned from this material can be pulled through a wedding ring, since the threads are so thin and silky.

Saw-toothed Pen Shell
(Atrina serrata)
This shell is quite large and thin and has many crowded ribs. It is horny and scaly. The color varies from green to brown. This species grows to 11½ inches.

Rigid Pen Shell (Atrina rigida)
This pen shell is very dark, ranging from deep purple to black. Inside, it is pearly and iridescent. Sometimes a rigid pen shell is smooth; others have high spines on the ribs. It grows to 12 inches.

Naked Pen Shell (Atrina seminuda)
The naked and the rigid have a lot in

common, so you may have trouble telling the difference until you examine the insides. In the rigid, the muscle scar extends into the upper edge and into the pearly area. In the naked, the muscle scar is below the upper edge and the pearly area. Although this shell's range extends from North Carolina to the Caribbean, few, if any, are found in Florida.

Atlantic Geoducks

Atlantic Geoduck
(Panope bitruncata)

This species is rare enough that you will have a real find if you discover one. But it can be done, although the species was believed to be extinct until recent years. This pure white clam is found from the Carolinas south. The shell is well inflated, although one end is truncated. Beaks are prominent, and the surface feels smooth, although it is adorned with fine lines. It grows to more than 7 inches.

Oysters

Under the heavy shell, so common along the banks of swashes and inlets in the Carolinas, is the fleshy body of the oyster—the basis of large and important fisheries in Carolina estuarine waters. Seafood restaurants along the coasts serve thousands of pounds of oysters each year.

Oysters attach themselves to rocks or to other oysters and stay there the rest of their lives. A group of oysters is called an oyster bed. As oysters cannot tolerate the salinity of sea water, they are more abundant in estuarines and inlets where salinity is less than in the open ocean. However, oyster shells are common on the beaches;

they are washed to sea and then back to the tideline among other shells.

Oyster shells are lined with tissue called a mantle, which grows from each side of the body. The mantle secretes layers of a limelike substance that forms the shell. Scientists estimate that certain oysters live 20 years or longer.

Eastern Oyster
(Crassostrea virginica)

Very early in life this oyster selects a hard object and cements itself to it. Older specimens may be an inch thick, and they grow to 10 inches. The shells vary in shape, depending on the base on which they grow, but, generally, they are long and narrow and moderately curved. Color is lead gray or purple. This oyster is rough, frequently bearing scars, stains or seaweed.

Sponge or Soft Oyster
(Ostrea permollis)

This oyster has a thin, translucent, rather smooth shell. It is yellowish, and it grows to 1 to 2 inches. The surface is wrinkled with irregular ridges.

Horse Oyster *(Ostrea equestris)*

This species is also known as the crested oyster. The shell is a little more oval than other oyster shells. The color is a dull brown, and the interior is gray green. This species is not used commercially.

Atlantic Wing Oyster
(Pteria colymbus)

The most unusual feature of this brown oyster (nearly 4 inches) is a winglike extension from the hinge. The inside is pearly white. This shell is said to be a pearl oyster, but should you find a pearl here, it will likely be too small to have commercial value. This oyster holds fast to sea whip strands. When storms dislodge the sea whips and wash them to shore, the oysters hold on for dear life.

Kitten's Paws

A kitten's paw is a tiny oyster shell. These shells are fan-shaped, and the six or seven folds radiating from the beak make them resemble the paw of a kitten so much that the name is perfect. Some of these little animals cement themselves together, forming a small box, and they are not easily separated.

Kitten's Paw (Plicatula gibbosa)
Radiating surface ridges on this fan-shaped shell (1 inch) look like the forefeet of a kitten just before its claws dig into something. They are white with reddish brown or pink markings on the ridges.

Lucines

Lucine is a creature which finds life in the Carolina coastal aquatic world to its liking even though the rumor is that it is tropical. There are nearly 200 species of lucines. The two valves have almost the same size and shape, and they are usually round.

Miniature Lucine (Lucina amianta)
This little round shell, less than an inch long, is well inflated and tough. It is decorated with eight or nine radiating ribs and seems merely brushed in concentric lines. It is pure white.

Pennsylvania Lucine
(Lucina pensylvanica)
This white shell (1 to 2 inches) is circular and strong, and its most unusual characteristic is a deep fold beginning at the beak and extending to the margin. The fold makes the bivalve appear to be almost a shell within another shell. Concentric ridges decorate this lucine, which is often found in sea drift from Cape Hatteras south.

Many-lined Lucine
(Lucina multilineata)
This shell is nearly a twin to the miniature lucine, except that it is smoother and a little more puffed out. It is white and only ¼ inch long.

Comb Lucine (Lucina pectinata)
Uneven concentric lines decorate the surface of this yellow orange shell. It is a little over 2 inches, and the wide hinge plate bears either teeth or the sockets into which they once were a perfect fit. So depending on which of the valves you are observing, you will see either teeth or sockets.

Basket Lucine (Lucina nassula)
The ends of 20 radiating ridges fringe the edge of this white, round shell. With both radiating and concentric ridges, this shell (about ½ inch) is showy. It is sometimes called woven lucine. Either name, basket or woven, is a good description of the sculpture of this shell.

Buttercup Lucine (Anodontia alba)
The buttercup is round, well inflated and white. Striking yellow orange tints on the side give this 2-inch bivalve its name.

Philippi's Lucine
(Anodontia philippiana)

Philippi's is much like the buttercup except that it is white inside as well as out. It grows to 4 inches.

Dwarf Tiger Lucine
(Codakia orbiculata)

If you are lucky enough to find this shell with both valves intact, look at it from the side. From this angle it is heart-shaped. Examining a separate valve, you will see that the beak is pointed and teeth are well-defined and sturdy. It grows to ½ inch and is usually white, though it sometimes has touches of yellow or pink.

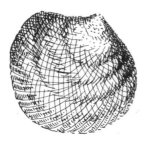

Cross-hatched Lucine
(Divaricella quadrisulcata)

White and shiny, the cross-hatched has tiny grooves that gave it a faint herring-bone pattern. Nearly an inch long, this shell is swollen, almost globe-shaped. It is an elegant shell and a common one on Carolina beaches.

Dentate Lucine *(Divaricella dentata,*

Another white lucine, this one (1½ inches) is circular and plump. It has scalloped edges.

Jewel Boxes

For the most part, jewel boxes are brought to shore by fishermen who have been seining offshore. Their shape is irregular, and the valves are of unequal sizes. Jewel boxes are handsome and hardy, colorful and scaly, and always a joy to find.

Leafy Jewel Box
(Chama macerophylla)

This shell (3 inches) is as leafy as lettuce.

It comes in various colors, including yellow, purple, orange and pink. Both valves are lacelike, ruffled. The quieter the waters in which it grows, the longer the ruffles. It looks somewhat like an oyster.

Corrugated Jewel Box
(*Chama congregata*)

There is no leafy appearance here. The surface is decorated with some elevated, radiating ridges crossed by some concentric growth lines. This shell (1 inch) is usually white with a dull brown or red tone.

Spiny Jewel Box (*Arcinella cornuta*)

Just as the name says, this shell (1½ inches) is spiny. It is thick, rectangular and white with brown stains. If you cannot find a free shell, you might locate this species holding to other shells or rocks. Six to eight ribs embellish each valve.

Cockles

Cockles were immortalized in the nursery rhyme:

Mary, Mary, quite contrary,
How does your garden grow?
With silver bells,
And cockleshells,
And pretty maids all in a row.

Cockles became widespread throughout the world about 65 million years ago. As they evolved, they developed stronger ribs that today make them resemble ruffled potato chips. Although these bivalves are eaten in Europe, they are rarely consumed along the Atlantic coast. There are more than 200 living species of cockles.

Cockles are equivalve and when viewed from the side are heartshaped. Edges of the shells are scalloped. They are abundant along Carolina beaches and especially on the banks of the Intracoastal Waterway near North Myrtle Beach.

According to slave narratives on file at the Library of Congress, one little slave girl living on a plantation on the coast of South Carolina carried a cockle shell with her at all times. The shell was a kind of security blanket for her, and she also used it as a spoon while eating her meals.

The design of the cockle has inspired shell-patterned silverware, china, cloth and bathroom fixtures. This motif also abounds in jewelry.

China Cockle
(Trachycardium egmontianum)

On this shell (about 2½ inches) scales protrude from the 27 to 31 ribs, inspiring the name. The sides of the shell fall back and give it a somewhat oblong shape. The outside is white or gray; the inside is pink and purple. The outside may be splotched with brown or purple.

Yellow Cockle
(Trachycardium muricatum)

Spines are evident on the 30 to 40 ribs which radiate from the beak area to the edge of this shell (1½ to 2 inches). The outside is creamy white with patches of brown or red, and the inside is usually white tinted with yellow.

Spiny Paper Cockle
(Papyridea soleniformis)

The shell (1 inch) is thin and flat. Short spines adorn the sturdy ribs radiating near the margin. It is white with a tinge of pink, sometimes orange, heavily splotched with brown inside and out. The interior is glossy.

Giant Atlantic Cockle or Great Heart Cockle (*Dinocardium robustum*)

Here is a shell that is thick and sturdy and deeply inflated. About 35 ribs radiate on the exterior, and the interior is also grooved. This shell (3 to 5 inches) is rosy pink or white, sometimes yellowish brown. It is stained with brown and purple bands. Beaks are rounded.

Atlantic Strawberry Cockle (*Americardia media*)

The sides of this thick shell are squarish, and the posterior margin is truncate, forming a slope on that end. The outside is creamy white, and the inside is sometimes checkered with rose and purple. If you count the ribs on this 2-inch shell, you will find 33 to 36 radiating from the hinge. Collectors have little difficulty finding plenty of these.

Quahogs (clams)

The word quahog (CO-hawg) is based on an Indian word meaning bivalve. This clam, like the oyster, is important as a commercial seafood product.

Quahogs were used by American Indians as "wampum," their hard cash. This money was made from the purple portion of the shells. Quahogs were also a staple in the Indian diet, and shell mounds along the coast attest to Indian cookouts.

According to a recent article in *Pawley's Island Perspective*, up to 40 bushels of clams are taken from the creek at Pawleys Island each day. Wildlife officials say that if the taking of the clams isn't curbed, the shellfish population will be severely depleted in few years. An average clam digger can gather 300 to 500 clams in about two hours.

Quahog or Hard-shell Clam
(*Mercenaria mercenaria*)

Narrow concentric folds and growth lines decorate this shell. When fully grown (5 or 6 inches), it is heavy, thick and gray white with a deep purple spot on the inside. This shell occasionally produces purple or white pearls, but having no luster, the pearls look like beads.

Cures for the many types of cancer may still be some years away, but it just may be that "the cure" will at last come from the *Mercenaria mercenaria* clam.

A potential anticancer agent in this clam was discovered by Dr. Arline Schmeer of the AMC Cancer Research Center and Hospital in Lakewood, Colorado. She first identified the agent in 1962 and named the clam-liver extract "Mercenne." Dr. Schmeer is legally forbidden to dispense the drug, which as yet is unproved.

Whether or not the hard-shell clam proves to contain a cure for cancer, it will remain a joy to shell collectors and the yummiest of seafood morsels to clam diggers.

Southern Quahog
(*Mercenaria campechiensis*)

This shell (2 to 6 inches) is pure white with no purple stain. The whole exterior is covered with concentric ridges. It is not as common as *Mercenaria mercenaria*.

Venus Shells

Venus was the goddess of love and beauty in Roman mythology. The Greeks called her Aphrodite and said that she was born from the foam of the sea. Is it any wonder, then, that these shells are interesting and heavily decorated?

Cross-barred Venus
(Chione cancellata)

Concentric ribs decorate this shell (½ to 1¼ inches), and some radiating ridges are under them. This shell is gray white, occasionally with brown splotches, and is roughly triangular. The inside is stained with purple.

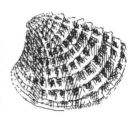

Lady-in-waiting Venus
(Chione intapurpurea)

The concentric ridges on this 1½-inch shell are more closely set than on the cross-barred Venus, and there are also more ridges. This creamy white shell has brown spots, but the inside is smooth and purple.

Gray Pygmy Venus *(Chione grus)*

This little shell (less than ½ inch) is well sculptured with radiating ridges crossed by concentric lines. It is more oblong than round and is gray white with touches of pink or orange. A purple band decorates the inside.

Imperial Venus *(Chione latilirata)*

This is a classy shell (1 to 2 inches) with rounded concentric ridges that look almost like tiny shelves. The outside is tan with lavender splotches. It is solid and sturdy, and it enhances any collection.

Gem Venus Clam *(Gemma gemma)*

White with lavender or purple accents, this tiny clam (⅛ inch) is lavishly endowed with fine, concentric furrows. It lives on sand or mud flats above low-tide level, and shells are abundant on beaches.

Codfish Venus *(Pitar morrhuanus)*

You probably will not find this species in

South Carolina, but it has been collected in North Carolina. A rather hefty shell (1 to 2 inches), it sports irregular, concentric growth lines and is gray with rust stains. Although this shell looks something like a quahog, it is not as solid and lacks the purple stains.

Lightning Venus *(Pitar fulminatus)*
The lightning Venus is much like the codfish Venus except it is chalky white and has brown zigzag markings. It is oval and plump.

Gould's Wax Venus *(Gouldia cerina)*
This tiny, triangular-shaped shell (½ inch) is yellow white and has concentric lines as well as radiating lines.

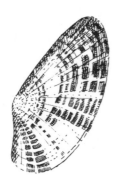

Sunray Venus *(Macrocallista numbosa)*
Storms wash in great quantities of this shell, which can grow to 6 inches. If you see one before the sun bleaches the brilliant colors, you are in for a show. Gray and coral stripes are crossed by other colors, mostly lavender and brown. An excellent clam chowder is made from sunray Venus, which is commercially harvested in Florida.

Elegant Venus *(Dosinia elegans)*
Just as elegant as the name implies, this 3-inch species is pure white, circular and compressed. Concentric lines are closely spaced: they number about 25 per inch in adults.

Disk Shells

Disk Shell *(Dosinia discus)*
This 3-inch shell is trim and neat and

much like the elegant Venus. You'd hardly notice it, but the surface is adorned with tiny concentric lines. The white surface either has or once had a thin, yellowish layer which peels away to reveal a glossy finish.

Scallops

If there is a favorite shell among collectors, it must be the scallop. Scallops may be best known as the trademark of Shell Oil, but the shape was used decoratively long before Shell drilled its first well. The design of the scallop has been used in art since Biblical times.

At an archeological dig in Israel in 1981, a Duke University professor of religion discovered an ark which held sacred writings. This ark was the oldest Biblical chest found up to that time, and it featured scallop shell decoration.

The scallop is a common symbol in coats of arms. The Crusaders of Europe in the eleventh, twelfth and thirteenth centuries employed the shell as a badge of honor.

Scallop valves are not equal. While one is curved, the other is rather flat. A row of tiny eyes fringes the mantle, each eye complete with cornea, lens and optic nerve. Scallops are brilliantly colored and are common to all seas. By fluttering along, spouting a little jet propulsion, they earned the nickname, "butterflies of the sea."

Scallops could get by on their looks alone, but they also are famous as tasty morsels on seafood platters. Some scallop shells are found on beaches, and many excellent specimens are found at excavation sites and in the banks of the Intracoastal Waterway. But for the most part, they are brought to shore in fishermen's nets.

Ravenel's Scallop *(Pecten raveneli)*

One valve of this 2-inch shell is quite flat with irregular marking, and the other is cupped and decorated with 25 strong, grooved ribs. One valve has dark markings. This shell is usually pink or purple, but sometimes it is creamy yellow.

Atlantic Deep Sea Scallop *(Placopecten magelanicus)*

If you find one of these south of Cape Hatteras, you will be lucky indeed. Valves are smooth, large and solid, and one is reddish brown. The lower valve is nearly flat and pinkish white with a glossy interior. The surface is sculptured with many lines and grooves. Fishermen go offshore in search of this scallop which grows to 8 inches.

Zigzag Scallop *(Pecten ziczac)*

Fanning out to 4 inches, this species has about 20 strong radiating ribs. It is red brown. The upper valve is flat, while the lower one is deep and overlaps the upper.

Calico Scallop *(Argopecten gibbus)*

This scallop (1½ inches) has inflated valves that are about equal in size. On its surface are 19 to 21 radiating ribs and growth lines. It comes in many colors including orange, yellow, rose and brown. Although this species is taken offshore by fishermen, it is also found on beaches. It is popular for making shell novelties.

Atlantic Bay Scallop *(Argopecten irradians)*

This common, edible scallop (2 to 3 inches) is drab gray or brown. It lacks the excitement of more colorful specimens, but it is important in the commercial fishing industry. The valves are rather swollen, and one has more color than the other.

Lion's Paw *(Nodipecten nodusus)*

This striking, desired-by-collectors species is bright red, deep orange or purplish red. The surface has large ribs with substantial, hollow nodules. It resembles the paw of a lion.

These shells are abundant in offshore waters, and although they don't wash up on the shore every hour every day, single shells can be found on beaches after storms.

Rough Scallop
(Aequipecten muscosis)
This 2-inch scallop is a shallow-water species. Its color ranges from pink to deep red, occasionally splotched with other shades. The small but robust shell has about 20 strong ribs, and scales adorn the ribs near the margin. Look for this one in tidal pools.

Angel Wings

These shells resemble the wings of an angel and are so white and fragile they seem to be made of baked egg white. This celestial wing cum seashell is sure to satisfy the most discriminating appetite for beauty.

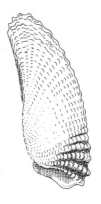

Angel wings live in the sand, often as deep as 12 inches, and some of them never come to the surface. They eat whatever food they can syphon down to their place of abode. The surfaces of both valves are highly sculptured. They have no hinge teeth.

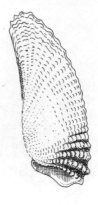

Angel Wing (Cyrtopleura costata)

Angel wing is the perfect name for this thin, brittle shell (5¾ inches) with its hinge near the top of the valves. Thirty beaded ribs crust these heavenly white shells. The radial sculpture is reflected in the glossy interior.

Campeche Angel Wing (Pholas campechiensis)

The name of this white shell (4 inches) means "lurking in a hole." It is almost flat, cylindrical in shape. You can recognize this one by a shelly plate that strengthens the upper part of the shell. It resembles the angel wing, but it is smaller and slimmer.

False Angel Wing (Barnea truncata)

See this one while it's alive, and you will see loose accessory plates atop the hinge area. This white shell (2 inches) has weaker and less scaly sculpture than other angel wings. You are not likely to find it without cracks and chips.

Wood Piddock or Striate Piddock (Martesia striata)

Usually pear-shaped, this shell (1 inch) is gray white and can sometimes be found on old, waterlogged boards. It bores with a long foot that stretches out. The valves are divided into sections by grooves extending from the beak to the edge.

Tellins

Tellins come in a variety of forms —small and large, round and oval, shiny and dull. They are found in all seas. They have long, much-used syphons. A tellin is a sand burrower, and you can recognize one by the twist to the right of the posterior end.

Speckled Tellin (*Tellina listeri*)

Dull surfaced and oval shaped, this shell (3 inches) is decorated in evenly spaced concentric lines. It is white with purple accents. The inside has yellow stains.

Alternate Tellin (*Tellina alternata*)

The anterior is round and posterior twisted in this triangular shell (1½ to 3 inches). It is glossy white and has concentric grooves. The posterior area is marked by a ridge that angles from the beak to the margin.

White-Crested Tellin (*Tellidora cristata*)

Four rows of heavy crests ridge and form teeth on the lateral margin of this 1-inch shell. It is compressed, and the ventral margin is broadly rounded. It is pure white.

Rosy Carnaria or Pink Scraper (*Strigilla carnaria*)

Solid and smooth, well inflated and round, this shell (1 inch) is pale pink outside and rose inside.

Crystal Tellin (*Tellina cristallina*)

You may find this species in South Carolina, but it would be surprising if it appeared on North Carolina beaches. The anterior end is rounded, and the posterior end slopes to a squared-off tip. This 1-inch shell is transparent, shiny white.

Sunrise Tellin (*Tellina radiata*)

Everyone loves this tellin, which is a polished creamy white with pink or yellow rays. The interior of the 2-to-4-inch shell is yellow. It's a natural for use in shellcraft novelties.

Macomas

Macomas are wedge shaped, very thin shells that lie buried in mud on their left valves, using their siphons to take in food particles from the surface of the mud and from the water.

Baltic Macoma (*Macoma balthica*)

This thin shell is oval to round in profile. The beak is central. It is 1½ inches long, and the pinkish white surface bears many concentric lines.

Phenax Macoma (*Macoma mitchelli*)

The beak of this oblong, ¾-inch shell is not quite central. It is dull white.

Surf Clams

Shallow water surf clams offer a wide variety of large, strong shells sculpted with growth lines and concentric ridges. You will see them in shallow clear water and on beaches, especially during fall and winter.

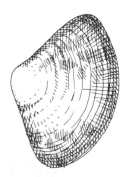

Atlantic Surf Clam
(*Spisula solidissima*)

This one is more common in North Carolina than in South Carolina. Its outline is roughly triangular, and it is yellow or white. The beak is large and central, and you'll see a deep cavity just under the beak. At nearly 5 inches, this is one of the largest bivalves found on Carolina beaches.

Fragile Surf Clam (*Mactra fragilis*)

A smoother exterior and broad round shape characterize this white shell (2 to 4 inches). Note the two radiating ridges on the slope of this species that loves sandy bottoms and shallow water.

Dwarf Surf Clam *(Mulinia lateralis)*
This little clam (1 inch) is puffed out and rounded, smooth and polished, and the color is nothing to rave about—gray, nondescript. An old favorite, it is sometimes called a duck clam.

Channeled Duck Clam
(Raeta plictella)
Pure white, thin and delicate, this clam is oval, and its surface is adorned with concentric ridges. It grows to 3 inches. The posterior slope narrows from the beak to the edge.

Wedge Rangia *(Rangia cuneata)*
This shell is thick, heavy and robust. Triangular in profile, the ¾-inch shell is white, and the interior is polished white. In life it wears a cloak of green or brown.

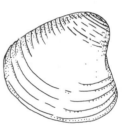

Soft Shell Clams

The soft shells are chalky gray and oval. The left valve holds a spoon-shaped plate to which the hinge cartilage is attached. Those little jets of water seen spouting from sand at the tideline come from this animal.

Soft Shell Clam or Long Clam
(Mya arenaria)
Moderately thick, this shell (3½ to 6 inches) ranges from white to gray. If you go "clamming" for food, this clam is one of the ones you are seeking.

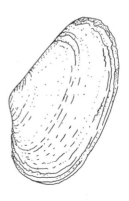

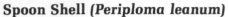

Spoon Clams

Spoons are small and delicate, and they have spoonlike pits in each valve.

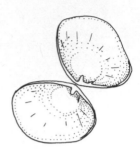

Spoon Shell *(Periploma leanum)*
As pearl white as one imagines the pearly gates, this shell (1 to 2 inches) has one valve that is flat; the other is round. A faint ridge is between the beak and the margin, and there is a spoonlike structure in each valve. This one is rarely found south of North Carolina.

Box Clams or Basket Clams

Basket Clam or Contracted Box Clam *(Corbula contracta)*
This tiny shell (½ inch) is off-white. It is inflated, triangular and sculptured with concentric ribs.

Swift's Basket Shell or Caribbean Box Shell *(Corbula swiftiana)*
Even smaller than the basket shell, this little shell (less than ½ inch) is triangular and white. From Cape Cod south you can find it.

Semeles

These oval shells with weak sculpture look much like tellins.

Cancellate Semele *(Semele bellastriata)*
Smaller than the purple semele, this one is oval and yellowish white. With both radiating and concentric lines, it is surprising that so much sculpture could be contained in this 1-inch shell.

Purple Semele (Semele purpurascens)
Another shell that bears fine concentric lines, this one (2 inches) is pale yellow with some purple splotches and zigzag lines.

White Atlantic Semele (Semele proficua)
This little creamy white bivalve (1½ inch) is a wanderer. Thin though it is, it creeps around on a powerful foot. Concentric lines on the surface are clear even though small.

Common Abra (Abra aequalis)
Oh so small at less than ½ inch, this shell still looks plump. It is white and slightly iridescent. The surface is rather smooth, although there are concentric wrinkles near the margin.

Tellin-shaped Cumingia (Cumingia tellinoides)
Sharp concentric lines decorate this ½-inch, thin, white clam. The posterior end is pointed, while the anterior end is round.

Nut Clams

Nut clams are triangular, and the two valves have nearly equal length and height. These small shells do not have the spectacular beauty of some other shells, but that's not to say they're uninteresting.

Common Nut Clam (Nucula proxima)
Small, robust, thick and wedge shaped is this shell (¼ inch). Notice the pearly interior and the teeth at the hinge area. It is white.

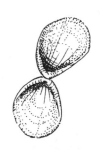

Pointed Nut Clam (Nuculana acuta)

Very small, only 1/5 inch, this nut clam is white. One edge of this shell veers out into a point. As tiny as the shell is, it bears numerous hinge teeth, and the surface is decorated with grooves.

Pandoras

Pandoras are a medley of flat and inflated valves: in each shell one valve is flat and another is inflated.

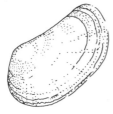

Three-lined Pandora (Pandora trilineata)

The posterior margin of this 1-inch shell slopes upward, and there is a hollow segment between the beak and posterior tip. This shell is white, the interior is pearly, and it is twice as long as it is wide.

Sand Clams

You'll go overboard for the sand clams found in the shallow waters of the swashes. Both valves are usually intact, and they are spectacular on the sand in the clear water. Single valves are found on beaches.

Divided Sand Clam (Tagelus divisus)

Yellow gray with purple rays, this species grows to about 1½ inches. It usually has a band of purple or brown near the edge of the shell. The beaks are located slightly above the center. Both ends are round, although the shape of the shell is elongate. Note the shiny interior of this fragile shell.

Vulgar Sand Clam *(Tagelus plebeius)*

This clam (from 1 to 3 inches) is elongate, and it has some coarse concentric lines. It is white, sometimes with yellowish tinge.

Razor Clams

Razor clams are satin smooth and elongate. They have parallel margins and both ends are bluntly rounded as in sand clams. Razor clams live in colonies in sand at the low tideline, and it is amazing how fast they can disappear into the sand. They move on a foot that when fully protruded is nearly as long as the shell. These clams are edible, and the name is appropriate: they look for all the world like old-time straight razors.

Corrugated Razor Clam *(Solecurtus cumingianus)*

This is probably the most common razor clam in the Carolinas. It grows to 2¾ inches, and the beak, like the sand clam's, is a little higher up than the center of the shell. It is white.

Jackknife Clams

You will find these long, slender shells on beaches in both Carolinas. They are slightly curved but still resemble a scooped-out popsicle stick. You will not find them much farther south than South Carolina. Measure the jackknife, and you will see that it is several times as long as it is wide.

Atlantic Jackknife Clam *(Ensis directus)*

The exterior of this 5-inch shell is green

or brown, and the interior is white or lavender. This species is six times as long as it is high. The sides are parallel, the ends square, and the elongated shell is slightly curved. Muddy sand provides it a secure home. It is very common in the drift of shells at the tideline, especially in the fall.

Green Jackknife Clam (Solen viridis)

This olive green shell is four or five times as long as high and is almost straight. You'll surely find this one in September.

Glass Clams

These clams have translucent and pearly shells, which have no hinge teeth. Most members of this family nestle in gravel or crevices.

Glassy Lyonsia (Lyonsia hyalina)

Extremely thin and pearly, this shell draws a collector naturally. Sometimes you will find glassy fragments rather than the whole shell, which is about ¾ inch, rounded and oblong. Often though, the whole shell is there. The surface is brushed in fine ribbing.

Jingle Shells

Here you have a seashell with one valve that is thin and glassy while the other valve is chalky. The glassy one is the one you will choose for your collection. It comes in many colors, including orange, hot pink and even black. While some jingle shells are shaped somewhat like a surf clam, others are crumpled and ruffled. As they grow, these shells work hard to assume the shape of whatever hard object they attach themselves to. Thus, they can be extremely irregular in shape.

Atlantic Jingle Shell
(Anomia simplex)

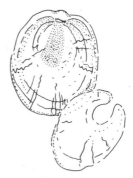

While one valve of this shell (1¾ inch) is inflated and almost transparent, the other valve is flat, strong and white and has a hole near the hinge. This bivalve attaches itself to rocks, oysters or other solid objects, but it is common on beaches.

Prickly Jingle Shell
(Anomia squamula)

The surface of this yellow gray shell is rough with radiating lines and scales. It is about half the size of the Atlantic jingle shell. The inside is purple and white.

Shipworms

Even after you have looked at a shipworm a solid 15 minutes, it is still hard to believe it is a seashell. They look like hardened gray worms. Shipworms specialize in hollowing tunnels in wood. As you can imagine, they are destructive pests to the U.S. Navy and other shipping interests.

Common Shipworm (Teredo navalis)

Although these may appear to be white, tubelike worms, they are really bivalves at the head of a tubelike structure. The shell is ¼ inch long, but the animal may be several inches long. They live in wood and are the enemy of wharves and wood products. After this animal attacks, timbers look like honeycombs, but it never intersects its neighbors' tunnels. Shipworm shells are found in coastal waters

Gould's Shipworm (Bankia gouldi)

This species has a white shell much like the common shipworm's. The shell is a set of tiny cones connected to a central core. It is not quite as long as the common shipworm's shell.

Awning Clams

Awning clams are elongated and inflated. They get their name from the little awninglike fringe at the margin of the shell. They are not common shells on the beaches, but die-hard collectors keep looking until they find one.

Common Awning Clam
(Solemya velum)

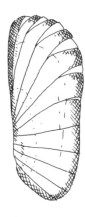

This greenish brown shell looks like an awning because radiating lines are split and extend beyond the edge, forming a little awning. You won't confuse this shell with any other—the awning is unmistakable. It is oblong, the ends are rounded, and it grows to 1½ inches. This shell should not be kept in a jar or tray with others, because the awning is fragile. Attach it to a card, or put it on cotton in a safe place.

Part Two
Gastropoda

Univalves (Gastropods) have one shell.

As with the bivalves, there is a soft body within the shell. A siphon extends from the body, and through the siphon the animal sucks in water or discharges wastes. A univalve also has a foot, designed for sprinting along rather than for digging.

Some univalves have teeth, known as *radular*. Certain conchologists (mollusk experts) classify some species by the character of the teeth and the number of teeth the shells possess. Univalves shred food with their teeth. They have a set of tentacles, used as feelers, and a kind of door (operculum) which they can open and close at will. More often than not when you find a univalve on the beach it will be an empty shell with no animal parts.

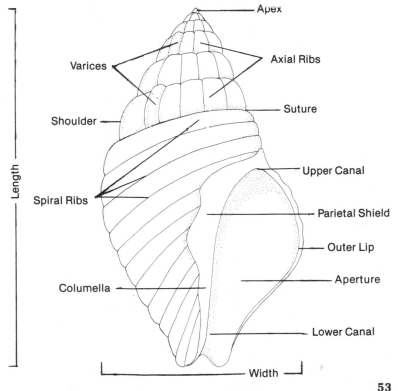

Slipper Shells

These oval, arched, tub-shaped shells are common on Carolina beaches, especially in the autumn. Look inside: there is an outgrowth that looks like a shelf.

Common Atlantic Slipper Shell
(Crepidula fornicata)
This species (2 inches) likes to cling to other shells and all but takes over oyster beds, smothering the oysters. It has a unique feature: a spire which is turned and which blends into the body whorl. These shells are off-white or tan and sometimes are splotched with chestnut brown. Their shape may remind you of a boat, and they have been referred to as "boat shells" and "quarter decks."

Convex Slipper Shell
(Crepidula convexa)
The outer surface of this ½-inch shell is wrinkled and reddish brown. The interior is bluish brown. Look for the shelly partition set deep in this arched-high shell.

Flat Slipper Shell
(Crepidula plana)
White inside and out, this shell (1½ inches) is rather flat but still has a hollowed-out shape. It is semi-transparent.

Thorny Slipper (Crepidula aculeata)
This 1-inch shell is brown or purple and bears spiny ridges. The interior is polished. Take note of the tip of the spire, which turns to one side.

Limpets

These shells are conical and oval, somewhat the shape of a Chinese coolie hat. Limpets are in the snail family, but they look about as much like a clam as a snail. They are not spiral at any stage of their growth. Generally, the many species of limpet shells are rather common on Carolina shores.

Key-hole Limpet (Diodora listeri)

This shell (1½ inches) is highly elevated and has an opening at the top. It is off-white and has large ribs crossed by cord-like lines.

Little Key-hole Limpet (Diodora cayenensis)

This one is much like the larger key-hole, except the surface sculpture is not as coarse and prominent.

Worms

There's nothing fancy here. No swirls of color, just unadorned shell tubes.

Knorr's Worm Shell (Vermicularia knorri)

When alive, this little ½-inch animal lives in jellylike globs in the sea, and it sometimes washes up on beaches attached to the jellies. The shell is amber brown. The coils at the spire are tight; they are looser as they wind away from the spire.

Turrets

Turrets are sometimes mistaken for augurs because both are slender and long,

and both Carolina species are about the same size. On the turret the outer lip commonly has a slit or a notch. The whorls are decorated with numerous spiral ridges.

Boring Turret Shell
(Turritella acropora)
This tiny, ¼-inch shell is yellow or yellowish brown. Tiny lines revolve around its spiral and sharp-pointed shell.

Eastern Turritella (Turritella exoleta)
Here again the spire is sharply pointed. This shell (2 inches) is creamy white with brown markings. You will find it from South Carolina south. It is surprising that up to 18 whorls can be contained in the slender shell.

Wentletraps

Wentletraps illustrate that bigger is not always better. These small shells come in unusual and fascinating shapes and make a fine show in any collection. They are usually white with strong ribs. The wentletrap is carnivorous, preying on sea anemones and coral. It exudes a secretion that turns purple and may have an anesthetic effect.

Angulate Wentletrap
(Epitonium angulatum)
There is something regal about this shell (about 1 inch). With a diamond on the high spire, it might be a miniature crown. It is glossy white, and each of the six whorls is decorated with about nine ribs.

Humphrey's Wentletrap
(Epitonium humphreysii)
This white shell is so much like the

angulate you may have trouble telling them apart. But this one (¾ inch) has a thick outer lip. Many axial ribs decorate the eight or nine whorls.

Banded Wentletrap
(Epitonium rupicola)
Brown bands spiral around this shell (about ¾ inch). It is a forager, searching over the sands of the ocean floor for small anemones.

Champion's Wentletrap
(Epitonium championi)
The ridges are fewer here than on other wentletraps and more widely spaced. The opening is oval, and the lip is slightly thickened. This ½-inch shell is dull white.

Augers

Augers are long and pointed. An auger's opening has a notch or canal where a siphon came out when it was alive. Augers (dead ones, of course) are found in sand near the tideline and sometimes back from the beach. They are widely used in shell art.

Common Auger (Terebra dislocata)
A tiny cord winds around the top of each of the 12 to 15 whorls of this slender, 2-inch shell. Note the slim, tiny lip by the small opening. This one may be gray, pink, orange or brown.

Fine-ribbed Auger (Terebra protexta)
Axial ribs are widely spaced on this auger, which, like the common auger, has 12 to 15 whorls. It grows to nearly 1 inch and is gray white or brown. The pillar at the base, around which the whorls form their spiral circuit, is twisted.

Concave Auger *(Terebra concava)*

A fancy shell, this one has beaded spiral rows. The design looks as though it came from an artist's easel. It is about 1 inch and is yellowish gray.

Horn Shells

Horn shells are ornate in sculpture. With ribs and grooves on the many-whorled shells, they do have style. This shell's round opening has a flaring lip and a siphonal canal. Most horn shells live in sand and feed on algae.

Florida Horn Shell *(Cerithium floridanum)*

The high spire of this shell (1½ inches) begins with fine lines that thread their way through rows of tiny beads. Teeth are within the opening of this shell. It is white with brown dashes.

Bittium Shells

These snails live in estuaries where the water is high in salinity, and they are often found in early summer.

Alternate Bittium *(Bittium alternatum)*

This shell is only 1/5 inch long, but it has six to eight rounded whorls that are decorated in a network of spiral lines and vertical folds, giving the surface a grainy look. The sand sometimes is so full of these blue gray shells it seems to be alive.

Variable Bittium *(Bittium varium)*

This one is like the alternate in appearance and color, but it is smaller.

Bubble Shells

Bubble shells are oval in outline. Think of them as being rolled up like a scroll. These snails burrow in sand for their prey. They are not too common in the Carolinas but occasionally are found on beaches.

West Indian Bubble *(Bulla striata)*
The outside of this shell (1¾ inches) is a mottled brown.

Tritons

Spindle-shaped tritons can be small, medium or large. With their highly decorated whorls, these shells add a special touch to a shell collection.

Tritons have been part of religious services around the world. In Japan they have served as church bells. Shinto priests called the faithful to services by blowing into a mouthpiece fitted onto the shell. (The spire was filed off to make a place for the mouthpiece.) In India the eerie sound of this shell (its musical quality has been compared to that of a foghorn) accompanied people marching to temple rites.

Hairy Triton Shell
(Cymatium pileare)
From South Carolina south you will find this gray or golden brown shell, which is embellished with bands of lighter and darker brown. The surface has ridges, and the lip reveals teeth. It grows to 5½ inches.

Doghead Triton Shell
(Cymatium moritinctum)
From South Carolina south you will see this shell with its inflated spire and boxy

shoulders. It grows to nearly 2 inches and is various shades of brown.

Trumpet Triton Shell
(Charonia variegata)

This shell (5½ inches) is high-spired with spiral grooves and a swollen body. The lip has folds. Very large and heavy, this shell is richly variegated in patterns suggestive of pheasant plumage. It is native from South Carolina south.

Distorted Triton Shell
(Distorsia clathrata)

There are ridges on both sides of the aperture on this 3-inch shell. Ribs are both axial and spiral, giving it a knobby appearance. It is white with touches of yellow, pink or brown.

Carrier Shells

It takes some investigating to see this shell for it is covered in other shells, stones and debris. Early in life this shell attaches its riders just back of the aperture. Carrier shells found in South Carolina usually select bivalves for their disguise; many of the chosen are cross-barred Venus shells. Fossil specimens of carriers have been found from the Cretaceous period, 100 million years ago. Hard as it may be to see, under all the freeloaders is a shell with a wide aperture.

Atlantic Carrier Shell
(Xenophora conchyliophora)

Measure this yellowish shell without the hangers-on and it would be about 2½ inches. This slow-moving snail is cone-shaped with concentric ridges.

Sundials

Sundial shells are round and solid, and they look outrageously close to being real sundials. If you think you are seeing only the top of the shell, look under the spiral cords and see the opening. It's all there. The hollow is large, encircled by a prominent beaded rib.

Common sundial
(Architectonia nobilis)
Creamy white with rust brown spots, this shell grows to 2 inches. It has five prominent beaded spiral cords that terminate at the lip.

Bifurrowed Sundial
(Heliacus bisulcatus)
This little sundial (⅓ to ½ inch) is not as fat as the common sundial, but the sculpture is strong with beaded cords. Two of the beaded cords are larger, and this is how it got its name.

Baby's Ears

Baby's Ear is a perfect name for this shell that's as smooth as a baby's skin. In addition, a line winds around into a circle that looks like a tiny ear, especially on the inside. When alive this univalve has a foot that is larger than the shell.

Common Baby's Ear
(Sinum perspectivum)
Small and thin is this shell, but it has a big opening. This off-white shell is brushed in many delicate lines. It grows to about 1¾ inches.

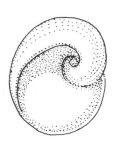

Maculated Baby's Ear
(Sinum macalatum)
The lines are not as prominent as on the common baby's ear, and the top is a little higher. It is brown with darker brown spots and grows to about 1¾ inches.

Turban and Star Shells

These shells do look like turbans worn by priests of India. They are bulky, and an outside layer of heavy sculpture covers a delicate iridescent underpinning.

Chestnut Turban Shell
(Turbo castanea)
Broadly conic, this shell is heavy and beaded. A drooping lip makes one side of the large opening wing out. It grows to nearly 2 inches and is orange, gray or green, splotched in brown.

Channeled Turban
(Turbo canaliculatus)
You will find this one from South Carolina, south. About five round whorls are decorated with deeply incised, revolving lines. It is usually greenish yellow, and it grows to 3 inches.

Engraved Star Shell (Astraea caelata)
Look at the base of the six or seven whorls of this species and see the scaly spines. This knobby shell is greenish white, sometimes with brown splotches. It grows to 3 inches.

Top Shells

Low and cone shaped, top shells have a delicate, knobby opening. They look like tops—toys that spin.

Mottled Top Shell
(*Calliostoma jujubinum*)

This pyramid-shaped shell is dark reddish brown, sometimes yellow brown, and it grows to 1¾ inches. The exterior has tiny, beaded spiral cords. Its deep hollow is edged in beads.

Beautiful Top Shell
(*Calliostoma pulchrum*)

Spiral beaded ridges are strong in the sections where the whorls are nipped in. This shell (½ inch) is creamy white.

Sculptured Top Shell
(*Calliostoma euglyptum*)

This top is 1 inch high and 1 inch wide, and it has five or six whorls. It is pinkish brown, variegated with white.

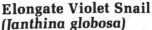

Violets

Violet snails are decorated in shades of lavender and purple. If they are pestered, they jet a purplish fluid. Their whorls are round and inflated, and the lip at the opening hangs down widely.

Common Violet Janthina
(*Janthina janthina*)

This fragile shell (1 3/5 inches) is adorned in shades of purple, pale nearer the spire, deep purple below. The surface of the three or four whorls bears fine lines. Although it is smooth, it is not glossy.

Elongate Violet Snail
(*Janthina globosa*)

Larger than the common or the dwarf, this violet snail grows to 1 inch. Its lavender shell has a big opening that sports an angular lip.

Periwinkles

This relatively tiny shell's bumps and ridges are molded by tides and sands. Periwinkles are eaten in Europe, but not here.

Marsh Periwinkle (Littorina irrorata)

Gray white with purple streaks, this 1-inch shell has deep grooves on the surface. The inner chamber is full-blown.

Moon Snails

Moon snail shells are low, globular and decorated with color, sometimes in zigzag lines, rather than in beads and spines. A moon snail has a long foot which keeps it mincing along. Almost any little animal in a bivalve becomes food for this univalve, which bores through the shell with its snout. Many of the holes you see in shells were drilled by these predators. They even attack their relatives. In somewhat the same manner as on the baby's ear, a well-toned line curves around on moon snails, making a sculpture that is more like an eye than an ear.

Colorful Moon Snail
(Natica canrena)

This shell (about 2 inches) is smooth and shiny. Its most dazzling feature is its large body whorl. Blue white, it is highlighted with zigzagged tints of brown.

Miniature Moon Snail
(Natica pusilla)

A small moon, less than ½ inch, this shell is glossy white or tan.

Northern Moon Snail (Natica clausa)
You may not find this moon (1 inch) south of North Carolina. It doesn't have much color, as it is usually covered by ivory white deposit.

Double Moon Snail (Polinices duplicatus)
A purplish shelly layer covers the umbilicus of this shell (2⅓ inches), which can have a low pyramidal or depressed oval shape. It is tan, sometimes blue gray and is also known as the shark eye.

Milky Moon Snail (Polinices lacteus)
This moon grows to 1 3/5 inches. It is milky white.

Hero Moon Snail (Lunatia heros)
A thin, puffy shell is this one. Its large body whorl is brown with highlights of blue. Inside it is glossy, polished. At 4½ inches, this is the largest moon snail found in the Carolinas.

Cowries

Cowries come from a respected family of attractive, popular members of the shell aristocracy. In India cowries have decorated the trappings of horses and elephants. Marco Polo saw them being used as money in China in the thirteenth century. They have been used as good-luck charms in the Pacific islands. They are brilliant, glossy and well-inflated. Their most noted feature is the long, narrow opening with lips that reveal evenly spaced teeth. Some species of cowries pass hands as money in the South Seas.

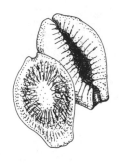

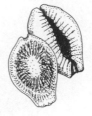

Yellow Cowrie
(Cypraea spurca acicularis)

The foundation of this 1-inch cowrie is white, and the top is speckled in orange and gold. This species is common from South Carolina south.

Helmet Shells

Helmet shells feed on sea urchins and sand dollars, and in many parts of the world the larger helmets become food in turn for people.

Reticulated Cowrie-helmet
(Cypraecassis testiculus)

This shell is found from North Carolina, south. It grows to nearly 3 inches, and the upper surface is decorated with brown spots. The shield and outer lip are orange. A body whorl makes up most of the shell.

Emporer Helmet Shell
(Cassis madagascariensis)

This helmet shell is a glossy creamy white with a latticelike network of spires. It is rare in the Carolinas. It grows to 14 inches.

Scotch Bonnet
(Phalium granulatum)

From all the seashells native to the shore of North Carolina, the Scotch bonnet was chosen as the official seashell of the state by the N.C. General Assembly in May, 1965. North Carolina was the first state to designate an official state seashell. The assembly chose this shell in memory of the Scotch settlers in North Carolina.

The Scotch bonnet (2 2/5 inches) is strong, well inflated and sculptured in grooves and ridges that have uniform squarish brown markings. The inner lip is glazed, and the outer lip is thick and finely notched.

Your best bet for finding a Scotch bonnet is to search the sea drift after storms or high winds. Finding a Scotch bonnet with its special beauty moves collectors in a way many other shells do not. Many Scotch bonnets are faded, but when the color is gone, the sculpture lingers on.

Margin or Rim Shells

These shiny shells consist mostly of one large body whorl. The outer lip is thick. American Indians found these shells on oysters, filed them off, and strung them to make jewelry. The jewelry was traded from tribe to tribe. They also used margin shells as money, which they called "roanoke."

Golden-lined Margin Shell
(Dentimargo aureocincta)
Two orange bands work their way around the ivory background of this pear-shaped shell. It grows to only 1/6 inch.

Plum Margin Shell
(Prunum apicinum)
Very glossy and cone shaped, this shell (½ inch) has an outer lip that is thick and strong. On a background of yellow orange, this shell has three bands of a darker hue.

Dewey Margin Shell
(Prunum roscidum)
This shell (¼ inch) has a pink background. If you look closely, you can see three bands of a slightly darker shade of pink.

Handsome Margin Shell
(*Prunum bellum*)
Glossy white, this tiny shell (¼ inch) has a thick outer lip and no spire.

Little Oak Margin Shell
(*Volvarina avenacia*)
This white shell has a creamy yellow shade at about the midsection of the body whorl. It is tiny at ½ inch.

Olives

These shells, favorites with most collectors, lie scattered about in the sea drift on Carolina beaches. They are especially noteworthy in that the body whorl makes up the shell except at the tip of the spire, where there are lines and furrows. Olives are shiny, and their aperture is narrow and long.

The colonists who settled at Jamestown, Va. recognized the natural beauty of olive shells and used them in making jewelry and ornaments.

Lettered Olive (*Olive sayana*)
This common shell grows to 2½ inches and is elongate, smooth and shiny. It is usually tan with purple or brown markings if the sun hasn't bleached it. The spire is short, and there are four or five whorls, with sutures deeply incised.

Variable Dwarf Olive
(*Olivetta mutica*)
A well-projected spire is the focal point of this shell (about 2/5 inch). Somewhat oval in shape, it has a creamy white exterior embossed with three bands of rust.

Flowery Dwarf Olive
(Olivella floralia)
Blue sometimes tints the white background of this slender olive that is less than 1 inch. The tip of the spire is sharp, and this shell lacks shoulders.

Cones

Cone shells come in all sizes, and here again the body whorl makes up most of the shell. The opening is long and narrow. This shell is much desired by collectors.

Florida Cone (Conus floridanus)
The spire is sharp and high in this cone (1 inch). Brown bands encircle the white shell. There are seven or eight whorls, although the body whorl is the outstanding one. The aperture is long and narrow, notched at the suture.

Stearns' Cone (Conus jaspideus)
Well-defined knobs decorate the shoulders of this shell (1 inch or less), which is shaped much like the Florida with its pyramidlike spire. It is gray, decorated with brown splotches.

Cowrie Allies

Cowrie allies are long, slender shells. They are glossy with a little strip of an opening.

Common Simnia (Simnia acicularis)
Narrow and oval, this shell (about ½ inch) has a long aperture and narrow lip. It is usually a faded yellow or purple but glossy.

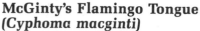

Single-toothed Simnia
(Simnia uniplicata)

Here again the color, pink or purple, is usually faded. This shell is a little wider than the common simnia, but like the common, it is elongate, almost cylindrical. The aperture runs the full length of the shell.

McGinty's Flamingo Tongue
(Cyphoma macginti)

Lavender and pink bring some color to this shell's off-white background. There are some brown spots near the margin. This one is rare and if found alive will be almost surrounded by the animal.

Volutes

This family of shells, prized by collectors, can be recognized by the broad spindle shape and the strong folds at the axial pillar around which the whorl coils. A volute is a prize in any shell collection, and a good specimen will sometimes bring up to $100 when sold.

Juno's Volute *(Scaphella junonia)*

There is much beauty in this creamy-white shell decorated with purple splotches. It grows to more than 5 inches. Note the folds and ridges at the edge of the opening. Although this one is rare in the Carolinas, it has been found here after storms. These volutes live in colonies on the ocean floor.

Tulips

Something about a tulip shell tells you that it's special. Dazzling in a shell display, tulip shells are large, strong and thick.

True Tulip *(Fasciolaria tulipa)*

Brown splotches and lines spiral around this shell with an ivory background. It grows to 6 inches and is strong and spindle shaped with a raised spire. The opening of the graceful shell is shaped like a raindrop.

Banded Tulip *(Fasciolaria hunteria)*

This is the species you are more likely to find on Carolina shores. Shorter than the true tulip by 2 inches, this tulip looks much the same with the smooth body whorl and brown spiral bands.

Tuns

Tun shells are white to brown with a varnishlike outer skin. Their surface is strongly ridged. They are somewhat similar to Scotch bonnets, but tuns are big and round, full-blown.

Giant Tun *(Tonna galea)*

This fragile shell grows to more than 6 inches. The lip has a thickened ridge, and 19 to 21 spiral ridges are widely spaced. Color ranges from white to tan.

Doves

These small, spindle-shaped shells are smooth or weakly sculptured. Doves come from a large family, and they are popular for jewelry making.

Well-ribbed Dove Shell
(Anachis translirata)

This little dove (¾ inch) has noticeable ridges. The surface is dull gray or brown.

Fat Dove Shell *(Anachis obesa)*

This shell is only half as large as the well-ribbed dove. It has brown bands around a white background and five stocky body whorls.

Nutmegs

Nutmeg shells are small to not so small, and the surface is latticed in sculpture. These univalves live from the low-tide line to depths of 4500 feet.

Common Nutmeg
(Cancellaria reticulata)

A cone-shaped shell that grows to more than 2 inches, this shell is creamy white with brown markings. Note the narrow ridges within the outer lip.

Frog Shells

The aperture of a frog shell has two canals for siphons. The shells are medium sized, usually with strong teeth or ridges on both inner and outer lips.

Chestnut Frog Shell *(Bursa bufo)*

Beaded lines circle this rare shell. It is dark brown and grows to 2¼ inches.

Fig Shells

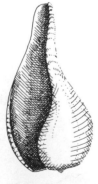

Members of this small family of shells are strong, elongate and have a big opening with a long canal.

Common Fig Shell *(Ficus communis)*

Brown spiral stripes on a creamy background are broken here and there. The spiral ridges are crossed by axial lines, unlike the pear whelk, a shell for which the common fig is often taken. The common fig grows to 4 inches.

Whelks

Few wares from the sea are more tempting to the collector than the whelk, an acknowledged sea treasure. Whelks live strenuous lives. Their favorite food is the animal that lives in the angel wing shell, and whelks dig down in the mud to get to them. By using the lip of its shell, a whelk can force these bivalves apart and feast on the soft bodies. It can reach a morsel six inches away by extending a ribbonlike attachment from its teeth.

Lightning Whelk
(Busycon contrarium)

This shell is easily recognized by its left-hand spiral. The shoulder of the body whorl is knobbed, and shades of purple streak a white background. The aperture may have a yellow tint. This shell often loses its color as it grows older. It grows to 16 inches and is much like the knobbed whelk except that the spiral turns to the left. Lightning whelks love to feast on quahogs as well as angel wings. In India and Tibet, any left-handed seashell was once considered sacred and was used in religious rites.

Stimpson's Whelk
(Colus stimpsoni)

You may think this shell looks like a tulip shell, and you are right. It grows to 5 inches and was named for a prominent nineteenth-century New England malacologist. It is fragile and sports weak spiral lines. This shell is rare, and if found, it may wear a brown outer skin.

Pear Whelk *(Busycon spiratum)*

The shoulders of this shell (5 inches) are smooth and slope more steeply than the knobbed whelk's. Lines decorate the creamy white surface. The suture, the junction where the whorls come in and go back out, is narrow. This shell is sometimes called the fig whelk.

Channeled Whelk
(Busycon canaliculatum)

The suture is wide in this shell with 5 or 6 turreted whorls. This species (8 inches) has strong shoulders. In young specimens, the shoulders are beaded. This shell is creamy yellow and is one of the most popular of all shells in collections.

Knobbed Whelk *(Busycon carica)*

The knobbed whelk grows to 6 inches. It is pear shaped, and while young its yellow gray surface is streaked in purple. The surface is smooth, but there are usually nine humps on the shoulder of the body whorl.

Gaudy Lesser Whelk
(Canthus tinctus)

This spindle-shaped shell (1 inch) can be purple, yellow brown or blue gray with white markings. If you look closely, you may see some surface sculpture.

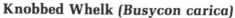

Conchs

Conch shells are a slice of the sea. Hold one to your ear. The sea whispers within.

A large body whorl takes up most of this shell. The aperture is long and narrow. If you find a conch shell that is well-worn, with tiny holes in the structure, that means it is an old shell. Any unusual shape makes the shell more valuable.

Florida Horse Conch
(Pleuroploca gigantea)
Under a rough coat of brown, this shell is gray white or coral. Heavy axial ridges are crossed by spiral cords. It grows to 2 feet.

Florida Fighting Conch
(Strombus alatus)
This conch (about 4½ inches) comes in shades of brown. The shoulders sport sharp knobs, all the same size.

Mud Snails

Mud snails which are also called basket snails, are cone shaped and less than an inch long. While some are smooth, others are sculptured with fine grooves. They are common in the Carolinas and are frequently found on unpaved roads within a mile of the ocean. They are popular for use in shell decoration. Still another name for the basket shell is dog whelk.

Bruised Basket Shell
(Nassarius vibex)
This chunky little ½ inch shell is gray brown daubed with purple. Count the surface ridges, and you will find nearly a dozen. Note the enamel covering on the inner lip of the opening and on a portion of the body whorl.

White Basket Shell
(Nassarius albus)
Leopardlike spots decorate this pale yellow shell (½ inch). It lacks a shield, and the body whorl and spire are about equal in length. This shell is well shouldered. The aperture is small, and the outer lip is thick.

Three-lined Basket Shell
(Nassarius trivittatus)
The suture is deep on this greenish white or yellowish white shell, and the surface is latticed in sculpture. The whorls look as if they are adorned with tiny shelves.

Mud Basket Shell
(Ilyanassa obsoleta)
The surface sculpture is weak on this 1-inch shell. The exterior is rough and dark brown. These snails live in colonies in sounds and inlets.

Rock Shells (Murexes)

Murexes are a rapture of ornate sculpture. Ribs, ridges and spines decorate the thick shells. Murex shells are not abundant in the Carolinas, but you can find them on the beaches.

Fossil murexes are fairly common in the banks of the Intracoastal Waterway near Myrtle Beach, S.C. This writer has seen none so beautiful as the tawny murex found by her son, Garry, in 1970 at the Intracoastal Waterway. (You can see this shell on the front cover of this book, pictured lying outside the glass jar.)

Murexes are active, carnivorous snails that live on rocky bottoms under shallow water. But like many species, they are usually dead and bleached white when you find them.

Tawny Murex (Murex fulvescens)
This shell grows to 7 inches. It's a treasure with its six to ten substantial ridges adorned with heavy spines. A milky-white background sometimes has brown or purple stripes. The aperture is wide. Note the wide syphonal canal.

Apple Murex (Murex pomum)

This shell grows to 2½ inches. The background is yellow white with brown splotches. The aperture is large, round and tinged with rose, and the outer lip is thick. This shell has strong ribs. Sutures at the five or six whorls are not distinct.

Pitted Murex (Favartia cellulosa)

This murex (less than 1 inch) is a tiny jewel. It has no spines on the gray white surface. The syphonal canal bends backward.

Blackberry Drupe Murex (Morula nodulosa)

Black bead sculpturing inspired the name of this spindle-shaped shell (less than 1 inch). You'll find this one from South Carolina south.

Lace Murex (Murex dilectus)

This murex (nearly 3 inches) is creamy white to tan. It is strongly ribbed and embellished with lacelike spines that are oh so fancy.

Thin Ribbed Murex (Murex leviculus)

This ¾-inch, light brown murex has shoulder spines that turn upward.

Oyster Drills

Thick-lipped Oyster Drill (Eupleura caudata)

The surface of this small (½ inch) but strong shell is rough with axial ribs and thin spiral lines. Note the teeth on the thick lip. The siphonal canal is nearly closed. It is white with purple bands. This species is a serious oyster predator.

Atlantic Oyster Drill
(Urosalpinx cinerea)

This little animal (under 1 inch) quickly drills into young oysters and feasts on the soft parts. This shell is too abundant for the oysters' peace of mind. The ash gray, spindle-shaped shell is decorated with ribs, ridges and spiral lines.

Part Three
Strange Creatures of the Sea

Most shell collectors collect other forms of sea life as well as species of the major divisions of the mollusk family. Some of the most familiar species of sea life you are likely to encounter while collecting shells are discussed here.

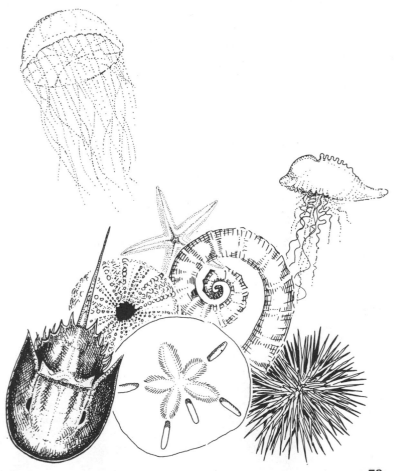

Sand Dollars

This echinoderm is also called "the Holy Ghost Shell." The design on one side of a sand dollar resembles a poinsettia, the Christmas flower. The marks on the opposite side look like an Easter lily, with a five-pointed star at the center, which could be the Star of Bethlehem. The five slits on the edge have been said to represent the five wounds in the body of Jesus when he was crucified. If you shatter the shell, the teeth in the center will tumble out. They look like tiny white doves, the doves of peace. From these symbols came the legend of the Holy Ghost Shell.

When alive, sand dollars have short spines that feel like velvet. These spines help them move in the sand under deep water where they live. They eat tiny animals and plants. Live sand dollars are brown, green or purple. You will be likely to find dead sand dollars lying on the beach, after they have been bleached white by the sun.

Sand dollars are relatives of starfish.

Starfish

This creature, like the sand dollar, is an echinoderm. Starfish usually have five arms, although some have more. If this creature loses a part of its body, it grows a new one.

Tubed feet allow a starfish to travel freely. When it finds a yummy bivalve, the starfish simply wraps its arms around the bivalve and pulls it apart. Oysters are among its favorite foods. When a starfish attacks an oyster, just after it forces the shell open it squirts in a chemical that makes the oyster relax.

If starfish were round, their yellowish brown surface with craters and dark and light zones could pass for the moon as seen in satellite photos. But they are star shaped, and they usually feel as hard as rock when you find them on the beaches.

Sea Urchins

Have you ever tasted sea urchin? Eggs taken directly from the sea urchin are served at the Strange Seafood Exhibition held each year at Beaufort, N.C. (The seafood festival, sponsored by the Hampton Marine Museum, is held on the third Thursday in August.)

Sea urchins are echinoderms and are relatives of starfish and sand dollars. They have quills that protect them and help them move along. Tiny tubed feet near the undersides of their mouths help them move and hold onto rocks.

When you find a sea urchin on the beach, it will be dead and will have lost its quills. If you shake the creature, you will hear five tiny teeth rattling around inside.

Horseshoe Crabs

Horseshoe crabs scamper over the sand flats, are caught, and are used in sea shell decorations. They are a favorite because of the long tail which protrudes from the plated, gray shell. The legs of a horseshoe crab are suggestive of those of a huge tarantula—hairy, black, stretching out, then withdrawing.

Sometimes you can find one as long as 12 inches, and this in itself makes an unusual wall decoration.

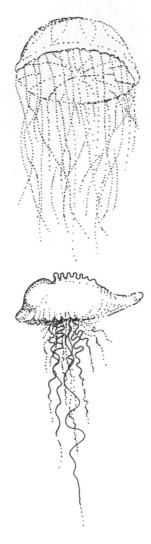

Jellyfish

If you see a colorless glob of jellylike substance lying on the beach, or a mass with a tinge of pink or orange, you have found a jellyfish. Their lifespan is about a year. They can be as small as 2 or 3 inches or as large as 6 feet across.

Jellyfish eat small sea animals. As they search for food, they propel themselves by opening and closing their mouths, squirting tiny jets of water.

Beware of this beast. A jellyfish has a tentacle that can stretch out to 5 feet, and it protects itself by stinging its enemy.

Man-of-war

The Portuguese man-of-war is dangerous. If you see a pink or purple, balloonlike substance on the beach, do not touch. It has a painful sting.

This is not one animal, but a colony of hundreds that attach themselves together to do their work. A pear-shaped portion of the animal floats on the surface, but tentacles can hang to 15 feet below.

Sharks Teeth

The teeth of about 14 species of shark are found on Carolina beaches. These are dusky, hexanchus, squatina, hammerhead, tiger, sand, corax, great white, mackerel, goblin, maki, hemipristis, bull and lemon. Color, shape and size of the teeth vary with the species of shark.

Nobody can say accurately just how old a sharks tooth is. Probably every sharks tooth you would ever find would be a fossil. All black and off-white sharks teeth are fossils. A fresh specimen is pure white, but these are rare.

Sharks produce an amazing number of teeth. In ten years a tiger shark may produce up to 24,000 teeth. It is possible that ancient sharks produced as many. A shark has hundreds of teeth at a given time. The inactive teeth lie flat against the jaws. But when a tooth is lost, one from the inactive group quickly replaces it.

Fossil forms are abundant on the coastal plain of the Carolinas. Heavy currents tend to loosen fossils bedded down on the ocean's sloping formations and pitch them to the beaches. Probably the most productive collecting can be done in bays and inlets.

In South Carolina there are fossiliferous beach deposits from the south up to Myrtle Beach. The south end of Pawleys Island is celebrated for its fine deposits, and Litchfield Beach isn't far behind in reputation. Edisto Beach, south of Charleston, is noted for its splendid fossil-bearing beach.

Fossil teeth found on the South Carolina Grand Strand are always on display at Trader Bill's Cove in The Gay Dolphin Gift Shop, near the Pavilion in Myrtle Beach. If you find a sharks tooth, Trader Bill will talk with you about it and even fashion a piece of jewelry displaying your find.

Ram's Horn

Remone Ram's Horn (*Spirula spirula*)

This pure white, 1-inch shell is divided into many chambers by partitions, and gas within the shell causes it to float.

Glossary

Anterior The margin or end of a bivalve to which the beak points. (The opposite end is posterior.)

Aperture The opening of the body whorl in a gastropod shell through which the animal's head and foot protrude.

Beak The beginning portion, or earliest part, of a bivalve shell.

Bivalve A seashell made of two valves.

Byssal Threadlike filaments that some bivalve shells use for support.

Calcareous A lime composition; shelly.

Carnivorous Flesh-eating.

Concentric Curving lines that form a semicircle around a common center.

Conchologist One who specializes in the branch of zoology dealing with the shells of mollusks.

Conical Cone-shaped.

Crenulate Scalloped or notched.

Cylindrical Having the form of a cylinder.

Dorsal At the back, toward the hinge of bivalve shells.

Echinoderm Any marine animal having a body wall stiffened by calcareous pieces that may protrude as spines.

Elongate Extended; lengthened; elongated.

Foot A muscular organ used in moving, sticking to a surface or digging.

Fossil Any remains, impression or trace of an animal or plant of a former geological age.

Gastropod Any mollusk of the class Gastropoda. Gastropods are called "the snails."

Hinge Where the valves of a bivalve are joined.

Inflated Puffed up; swollen.

Iridescent Displaying a play of lustrous colors like those of the rainbow.

Malacologist One who studies mollusks.

Mantle A fleshy membrane that covers the soft parts of a mollusk. It secretes the substance that forms the shell.

Margin Edge of the shell.

Mollusk Typically having a calcareous shell of one, two or more pieces that wholly or partly enclose the soft, unsegmented body. Comprises the bivalves and univalves.

Nodule A knoblike projection.

Parietal shield A covering on the inner lip of a gastropod.

Periostracum An outer covering on some shells.

Posterior Opposite of anterior. (See anterior.)

Quill Hollow spine.

Radiating Starting at the beak of a shell and fanning out; usually lines or ribs.

Radular The dental apparatus of gastropods.

Sculpture Impressed or raised markings on a shell's surface.

Siphon A tube beginning at the mantle.

Spire The upper whorls from the tip of the shell to the body whorl.

Suture The spiral line of the spire where one whorl touches another.

Tentacle A slender, flexible filament or glandular hair that extends beyond the shell.

Univalve A snail or gastropoda having a single shell.

Umbilicus A small hollow at the base of the body whorl of snail shells.

Valve One-half of a bivalve shell.

Ventral Underside.

Whorl In spiral gastropods, one full turn of the shell.

Bibliography

R. Tucker Abbott, *American Seashells, the Marine Mollusca of the Atlantic and Pacific Coasts of North America,* Van Nostrand Reinhold Co., New York, 1974.

R. Tucker Abbott, *Kingdom of the Seashell,* Crown Publishers, New York, 1972.

William K. Emerson and Morris K. Jacobson, *The American Museum of Natural History Guide to Shells,* Knopf, New York, 1976.

Warren N. Johnston, Editor, *The Pawleys Island Perspective.*

Kathleen Yerger Johnstone, *Sea Treasure,* Houghton Mifflin Co., Boston, 1957.

Kathleen Yerger Johnstone, *Collective Seashells,* Grosset & Dunlap, New York, 1970.

Percy A. Morris, *A Field Guide to the Shells of Our Atlantic and Gulf Coasts,* Houghton Mifflin Co., Boston, 1947.

Hugh J. Porter, *Sea Shells Common to North Carolina,* University of N.C. Institute of Marine Sciences, Morehead City, N.C., 1971.

Harold A. Rehder, *The Audubon Society Field Guide to North American Seashells,* Knopf, New York, 1981.

A. Hyatt Verrill, *Shell Collector's Handbook,* Putnam's, New York, 1950.

Index
Carolina Seashells

Index

East Woods Press Books

Backcountry Cooking
Berkshire Trails for Walking & Ski Touring
Campfire Chillers
Canoeing the Jersey Pine Barrens
Carolina Seashells
Carpentry: Some Tricks of the Trade from an Old-Style Carpenter
Complete Guide to Backpacking in Canada
Drafting: Tips and Tricks on Drawing and Designing House Plans
Exploring Nova Scotia
Florida by Paddle and Pack
Free Attractions, USA
Free Campgrounds, USA
Fructose Cookbook, The
Grand Strand: An Uncommon Guide to Myrtle Beach, The
Healthy Trail Food Book, The
Hiking Cape Cod
Hiking from Inn to Inn
Hiking Virginia's National Forests
Honky Tonkin': Travel Guide to American Music
Hosteling USA, Revised Edition
Inside Outward Bound
Just Folks: Visitin' with Carolina People
Kays Gary, Columnist
Living Land: An Outdoor Guide to North Carolina, The
Maine Coast: A Nature Lover's Guide, The
New England Guest House Book, The
New England: Off the Beaten Path
Parent Power!
   A Common-Sense Approach to Raising Your Children In The Eighties
Rocky Mountain National Park Hiking Trails
Sea Islands of the South
Southern Guest House Book, The
Southern Rock: A Climber's Guide to the South
Steppin' Out: A Guide to Live Music in Manhattan
Sweets Without Guilt
Tennessee Trails
Train Trips: Exploring America by Rail
Trout Fishing the Southern Appalachians
Vacationer's Guide to Orlando and Central Florida, A
Walks in the Catskills
Walks in the Great Smokies
Walks with Nature in Rocky Mountain National Park
Whitewater Rafting in Eastern America
Wild Places of the South
Woman's Journey, A
You Can't Live on Radishes

Order from:

The East Woods Press
429 East Boulevard
Charlotte, NC 28203